THE STITCHBOOK HANDBOOK

How to create fabric memory books

KIM EDITH

Welcome...

I'm Kim Edith, Stitchbook creator, and I'm here to guide you through the exciting process of making your first fabric memory book.

Stitchbooking is about telling your story in fabric, so each book will be unique, made using personal photos, fabric and text.

I will be introducing you to the main techniques that I use, and hoping to inspire you to create your own Stitchbook. I am passionate that there are no rules in Stitchbooking - so follow as much or little of these methods as you want!

You can also use as many textile techiques as you like, from patchwork and embroidery to fabric paint and cross stitch, there is no limit to what you can add to the pages. However, you don't need to be a sewing expert to make your book as there are lots of simple techniques you can use too.

I hope you make a book you can treasure for years,

Thanks,

Kim
Edith
x

CONTENTS

WHAT IS A STITCHBOOK?

A Stitchbook is a fabric memory book that uses family photographs and treasured textiles to tell a personal story.

Stitch Your Story

Everyone has a story to tell; and whether it's your recent holiday, the life of a beloved family member or a collection of your favourite things, this handbook will show you how to preserve those memories in a tactile and enduring way.

Blank fabric pages can be decorated with personal photographs and text, along with small pieces of treasured fabric, ribbon and embellishments. You can use scraps of favourite clothing, souvenirs picked up on travels or buttons from your grandmother's button box.

Photographs are transferred to fabric using a transfer paper which can then be sewn onto the pages, and text can be made using a variety of methods. Your pages can then be decorated to explore your theme and add narrative using scraps of memorable fabric, embellishments, buttons, badges and beads.

4

The Handbook:

In this book I will be talking about how to use my pre-made blank Stitchbooks, made with folding pages and binding rings. Most of the methods will also be transferable to other types of fabric book if you want to make your own. Feel free to adapt the instructions as needed to suit your book construction.

I will give you simple tutorials of my most used techniques as well as highlight others you might want to try out. Not all of the techniques will be described in detail, either because they are very simple and don't need further explanation, or are much more complicated and need some prior knowledge which is outside the scope of this book. Hopefully you will be inspired by some of the more complicated methods, and use them as a starting point for further research and experimentation.

I will also assume a degree of knowlege of the basics of hand and machine sewing, although you certainly don't need to be an expert to make a Stitchbook and there are many beginner friendly techniques to try. You can also stitch by hand or machine - my examples are a mixture of both, and most of the techniques explained here can be adapted to both methods of sewing.

Here I will be explaining how to create a memory book with photos and text, but you are not restricted to making photo albums – the blank books can be used in many different ways. Add fabric collage to create an art journal, felt, bead and Velcro to make a kids activity book, or use one as a sampler book to practice different stitches or organise fabrics or threads.

The Examples:

All of the images in this book have been made by me over the past 5 years, and feature my personal photos and memories.

If you want to have a look at some of the books in full, there are images and videos of these in the Inspiration tab on my website: www.stitchbookstudio.com

5

THE STITCHBOOK

Stitchbooking starts with a blank Stitchbook - a pre-made fabric book that you can stitch into. Each book is made with folding pages that allow you to take them out of the bindings to decorate. This means that all of your messy thread tails are hidden in between the pages.

Folding pages hide the messy wrong side

Left: Your messy threads at the back of your work will be hidden inside the folds of the page.

Having a pre-made book with removable pages is great because you can work on several different pages at one time, use a sewing machine to decorate and (as the hard part has been done for you) concentrate on telling your story.

This handbook is designed to be used in conjunction with one of my blank fabric Stitchbooks, and I will be describing how to complete your book using methods approriate for these types of books only. The Stitchbooks come in various sizes and different materials, including linen, cotton and felt. Any of these will be suitable for the methods outlined in this book, although you may have to adapt them for the very small ones.

HOW THE STITCHBOOK WORKS

It couldn't be easier to decorate your blank Stitchbook. The pages have been constructed for you and they remove from the binding rings easily so you can add your story.

To remove the pages:

1. Open the binding rings by locating the join in the metal and push out and apart.

2. Remove the pages from the rings.

To Decorate:

Open the page flat. You will add your design to the outside of the folded page.

Make sure the fold is open this way out

Add your artwork here

To reattach:

To replace the pages, thread the eyelets back through the binding rings in the correct page order and close the join in the rings by pushing together until they snap shut.

How to choose a Stitchbook

Consider the following things:

How much time do you have? The large Stitchbooks take much longer to complete than the smaller ones.

How many pages do you need? The books have between 8-12 pages and only some of them can have extra pages added. Make sure you choose one that has enough for you to tell your story.

What fabric do you want? You can choose a rustic linen, a crisp natural cotton or a coloured felt. Each suit a different aesthetic style. What do you want yours to look like?

THE STAGES OF MAKING YOUR BOOK

Parts of a page:

There are four main parts to a Stitchbook page, and this Handbook will go through how you can tackle each one of them.

Photo Transfers

Background

Text

Decoration

Your pages will be stitched together in layers; starting with the background layer (anything that will be behind your photos) and working up to the top layer of small decoration.

The typical order you would add elements in follows the chapters in this book:

Order of making

1. Decorate your backgrounds (p. 18)

2. Print your photos and sew on (p. 33)

3. Add your text (p. 43)

4. Add decoration and embellishment (p.56)

TOOLS:

The basic kit:

- Sewing machine
- Iron and ironing board
- Computer
- Inkjet printer
- Scanner (if you want to use non-digital photos)
- Fabric scissors
- Embroidery scissors
- Pins, needles and other basic sewing materials

Other tools used in this book:

- Rubber/ clear stamps and regular ink pad
- Pinking shears
- Erasable pen (air, water or heat erase)
- Paintbrushes
- Lightbox for tracing lettering
- Quilting ruler and rotary cutter
- Silicon coated paper (to protect iron-on vinyl from excess heat)
- Freezer paper (a paper with a plastic or wax coating on one side that can temporarily adhere to fabric)

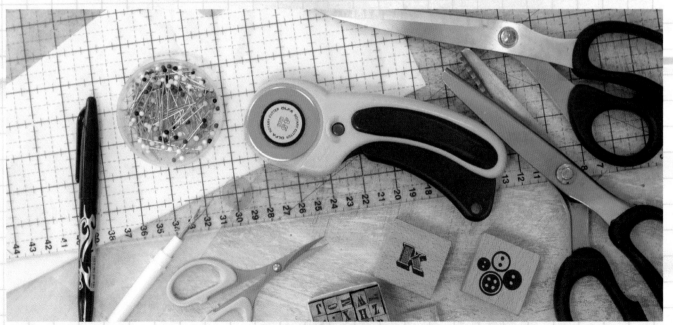

MATERIALS:

You will need:

- A blank fabric Stitchbook
- Photo transfer paper
- White cotton fabric for photo transfer
- Small pieces of fabric and felt for applique - to create backgrounds and decoration for your pages

Other materials used in this book:

- Embroidery thread - for lettering and decoration
- Buttons, ribbons, sequins and beads.
- Brads - these split pins can be found in the scrapbooking section of craft shops
- Fabric paint- for lettering and using with stencils
- Bondaweb - for attaching applique
- Iron-on Vinyl
- Temporary fix fabric spray glue

Above: A collection of fabrics, ribbons and embellishments ready to be used to decorate a Stitchbook about a trip to the Harry Potter Studios.

You can also use any other materials you have that will attach to the pages. You can add crochet flowers, use sections of hand painted silk or lace trims as well as any craft materials that can be adhered with fabric glue, such as thick card, wood or perspex shapes. Remember, as you are not going to wash the book, and it will not have heavy wear (like clothing or a quilt), there are very few restrictions in what you can add.

MATERIALS:
MEANINGFUL ITEMS

////////////////////////////

A good way to use fabric with sentimental value.

- -

A fantastic way to add nostalgia and personal meaning to your project is to include fabrics associated with specific memories and people.

You can either include the actual fabric (if you have it) - cut from an old shirt, baby clothes OR something that remind you of a specific person or time. This might be that your Nan always wore dresses made of a specific type of cotton, your Dad went through a phase of only wearing pink striped shirts, or a piece of lace that reminds you of a treasured childhood dress.

Stitchable Items:

You can include a range of stitchable items that you might have collected through the years such as:

- Guide/scout badges and patches

- Name tags from children's clothes

- Clothing labels from favorite, nostalgic or famous brands.

- Pieces cut from holiday souveniers such as hats and t-shirts.

CHOOSE A THEME

x x x x x x x x x x x

The first thing I always do for a new project is choose a theme to work from. This is a way of collecting ideas together, and will give a structure to your book. Choosing a theme at the start will inspire your colour and fabric choices, as well as influence what photos you should include.

A theme can be:

- A collection of ideas such as 'Things I like' or 'My Favourite People'.

- A narrative such as 'Baby's first year', 'This is your life' or 'Our 25 years of marriage'.

- A factual account of a family tree or ancestry.

- A record of a particular event such as a holiday or family reunion.

- A collection of images around one topic such as 'My Hometown' or 'The Sea'.

When I have chosen my theme I then look for fabric, embellishments and visual ideas that I think will fit with that theme and the photos that I want to include. If, for instance, I wanted to make a book about a trip to France I would try and find fabric that reminded me of the places I had visited, ribbons that had similar colours to my photos, buttons and badges that had French themed details. All of these collected items would form the base of my page designs.

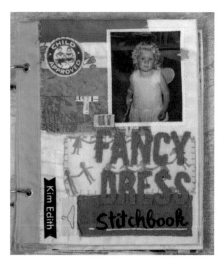

COLOUR & PATTERN

XXXXXXXXXX

You can use colour and pattern in your Stitchbook to further you story and enhance your theme.

How to use colours, textures and patterns:

1. Create a colour scheme:

Use a consistant set of colours to tie your narrative together and make the pages look like they are meant to be together as part of the same story.

2. Further your theme:

Use your colours to set the scene for your story. Use greens and reds for a collection of Christmas images or yellow and blue for seaside holiday photos.

3. Introduce the time period:

Different decades have specific colours and patterns associated with them. Use brown florals for pages featuring photos from the '70s or bright, bold prints to represent the '60s.

4. Highlight a specific idea:

Use colour and pattern to help explain what is going on in a specific photo. A page with a photo of a baby boy could be pastel blue, a photo from a pride parade could be accompanied by a rainbow background, a wedding photo could be framed in white with floral decoration.

This page is a love letter to Autumn after a walk in the woods. I wanted to match the colours to the photographs to have the immersive feeling of browns, oranges and golds that I had felt whilst walking through the trees.

PLANNING YOUR BOOK

You will probably want to plan out your story before you start, even if only a brief outline. This will allow you to space your pages correctly to be able to fit in everything you want to say.

I suggest breaking your story down into sections (the same amount as pages you have in your book) and working out what images and text will go on each page. I usually get out, or list, all of the photos I want to use and start from there.

It is also handy to refer to your planning sheet when making your pages so you know which order to put them (look for the eyelets on the left or the right). This is particularly important if your pages need to be in a particular order (chronological or grouped in themes).

You can find free printable planning sheets at www.stitchbookstudio.com/tutorials

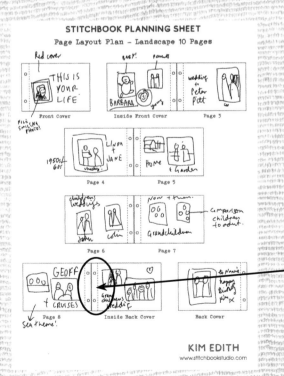

Below: Image showing page 9 of my book, and the corresponding part of the planning sheet. The elements have been added so the eyelets are on the left side of the page.

BACKGROUNDS

Index:

ADDING A BACKGROUND

The background provides consistency and coherence to different elements and set the tone of your page. Adding a background to your pages is a good excuse to use beautiful fabric, bold colours and to enhance the theme of your book. Search your stash for fabric with interesting patterns and shapes that help to tell your story. These could be of children's cartoon characters for a page about your grandchildren, or a floral print to match photos of your garden.

The background is the base layer of your page and all of the other elements - photos, lettering and decoration will be applied on top, so it will always be the first thing your sew onto your page.

There are several methods for attaching a background fabric to your Stitchbook. I have outlined two methods below for you to try out.

METHOD 1: RAW EDGES
XXXXXXXXXX

By far the simplest way to add a background to your page is to cut a piece of fabric the same size as your page and stitch to your book, matching the raw edges of the fabric to the edges of the page.

To attach, use a stitch that will control the fraying of the raw edge, such as a zig-zag machine stitch, a whip stitch or blanket stitch. You can even make a feature of this stitching by using bright or thick embroidery thread.

This method can be used with any of the techniques in this section. In this example I pieced together 3 pieces of fabric in a simple patchwork strip, then trimmed it to the same size as the page and stitched in using a machine.

METHOD 2: HIDDEN EDGES

X X X X X X X X X X X

A neater way to attach your background is to fold the fabric so the raw edges are tucked under and hidden.

The fabric gets hemmed at the left and right sides and tucked under the page at the top and bottom.

There are a few more steps here than the more simple method but worth it if you want your book to be raw-edge free.

How to create raw-edge free backgrounds:

1. Cut a fabric shape that is a couple of centimetres larger than the page on all sides.

2. Fold under the edge that will be next to the eyelets to the wrong side by 1cm and press.

3. Position the folded edge next to the inner stitching line on your page, and pin in place. Make sure it is centered so there is an equal amount hanging over the top and bottom of the page.

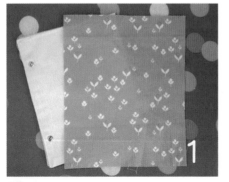

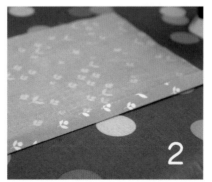

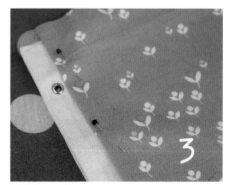

4. Stitch in place using a straight stitch on the sewing machine, staying close to the edge of the fabric (you may need to use a thin zipper foot to be able to stitch close to the eyelets).

5. Fold under the opposite edge by 1cm, to the wrong side, at the point it meets the fold in the Stitchbook page. Press.

6. Pin then stitch in place along this edge using a machine (for a visible line of sewing) or a whip stitch by hand (for an invisible line of stitching).

7. Fold the top and bottom edges under the page (this will sit in between the folded Stitchbook page). Press and pin in place.

8. Sew in place by hand on the back of the page, catching in only the inside layer of the Stitchbook page (so the stitches are not visible on the right side).

ONE-FABRIC BACKGROUNDS

//////////////////////////

The simplest background can also be the most effective.

- -

The easiest way to add a background is to stitch in one piece of fabric that covers the whole page.

If you choose the right fabric - one that adds to the theme of the page in pattern or colour, this is more than enough to create the base for a beautiful page. Remember you will be adding additional decoration later on.

Follow either method on page 19 or 20 to attach the fabric to the page.

These examples have a single piece of fabric as the base with additonal blocks of appliqued fabric and ribbons, buttons and sequins added later as decoration.

PATTERNED BACKGROUNDS

/////////////////////////

Use stamps and stencils to create patterns across your backgrounds.

- -

There are two easy ways to create your own patterned backgrounds: Using rubber stamp shapes or cutting your own stencils from freezer paper.

These methods can either be done straight onto the background of your book or (if you are afraid of going wrong) on a seperate piece of fabric which you can stitch in later.

Rubber Stamps:

Using the method on page 43 stamp out a pattern on your page. You can use coloured ink pads or fabric paint.

Left: A wooden cotton spool was dipped in fabric paint to create a makeshift stamp.

Right: A fish shaped clear stamp was repeatedly stamped across this page in coral coloured ink.

Freezer Paper Stencils:

X X X X X X X X X X

1. Draw out your design on the non-shiny side of the freezer paper. There are some templates you can trace on pg. 85.

2. Cut out the design with scissors or a craft knife to create your stencil .

3. Iron the freezer paper onto your fabric (shiny side down) to temporarily adhere.

4. Sponge fabric paint through the stencil.

5. When dry, remove the stencil by gently peeling back the freezer paper.

6. Repeat steps 2-4 to create a repeat pattern across your fabric.

You can also use the same method to create single images which you can cut around and use as deocrative applique patches (pg. 59)

If you don't have any freezer paper then sticky backed plastic will work in the same way.

You Will Need:

- Freezer paper
- Fabric paint
- An iron
- A sponge
- A craft knife or scissors

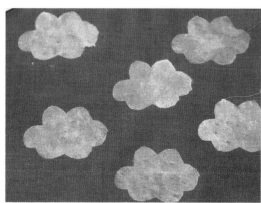

This page uses the stencilled clouds made on pg. 24 as a background to recreate the foggy atmosphere of the location. I purposely used a slightly transparent layer of fabric paint to represent the grey clouds, but you could add extra layers of paint to make the shapes opaque.

XXXXXXXX XXX

APPLIQUE BACKGROUNDS

////////////////////////////

Use blocks of fabric to add colour and pattern

Choose several fabrics and cut into blocks (I usually use rectangles as they are easiest to cut). Place the blocks on your page and move them about until happy. You also cut out your photos and play around with these at the same time to really get a feel for how the page will look. Attach the blocks to the background using a machine or hand stitch.

Tips:

- Try one block at an angle to create movement.

- Overlap the blocks to help your eye move around the page.

- You can leave the edges raw, use pinking shears to trim or turn the edges under.

- Cover straight joins with ribbon to hide raw edges.

- You can leave part of the background uncovered.

XXXXXX XXX

Right: I often use a strip of ribbon to hide the raw edges of fabric pieces. This pink velvet ribbon hides the raw edge of the floral fabric.

Applique blocks

The background of this page is made from just two fabric blocks. By placing one at an angle the page has more life and energy.

XXXXXXXX XXX

PATCHWORK BACKGROUNDS

//////////////////////////

Piece together simple patchwork blocks for a quality finish.

- -

Patchwork in Stitchbooking just means stitching blocks together before you add them to the page (rather than layering them like the applique method). It could simply be joining two pieces with a single straight seam.

Creating a pieced background is a great way to try out patchwork blocks on a small scale, and can be made with any type of patchwork from geometric, machine made designs to English paper piecing. I particularly like using patchwork to cover the front and back covers.

Create the patchwork first, then stitch into your book using either the method on page 19 or 20.

Left: Front cover made from hand-stitched hexagon English Paper Patchwork.

Right: Machine stitched patchwork using triangles.

Patchwork Photo Frame

This page is an example of how a piece of patchwork can add to a simple page design. I transfered this image onto the cream fabric, then pieced it together with some blocks in lines to create a frame. With only minimal extra decoration (text, running stitch around the image, logo), the page is complete.

XXXXXXXX XXX

PRAIRIE POINTS

////////////////////////////

My favourite technique for adding texture and depth to a page.

- -

These are an easy-to-make form of fabric origami made from small scraps of fabric. The points are made seperately then stitched to your page.

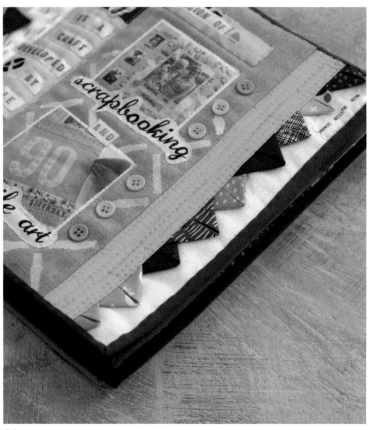

Tips:

You can also use prairie points in more inventive ways. Above I have stitched them behind a circular photo.

You can change the size of the points by using a smaller or larger square template.

How to make Prairie Points:

Use the template on pg. 85 to cut squares of fabric in your chosen colours.

1. Fold each square in half, wrong sides together. Press.

2. Fold one outer corners in to meet the raw bottom edge. Press.

3. Fold in the other corner to meet in the middle and form a triangle.

4. Add a tacking stitch at the raw edge to secure all of the layers together.

5. Position on the page - you can place them join up or join down.

6. Baste in position then stitch into a seam, or cover with ribbon or fabric.

7. Remove any visible tacking stitches.

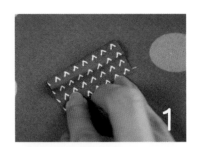

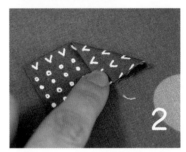

You Will Need:

- Scraps of fabric
- Paper template (print from page 85)

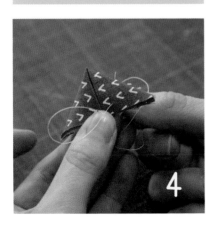

Prairie Points

The prairie points on this page add texture and colour to an otherwise simple page. It also helps to link the photo with the rest of this book by bringing in colours from my colour scheme that aren't shown in the image.

PHOTO TRANSFERS

Index

PHOTO TRANSFERS

///////////////////////////////

How to use photo paper to transfer your images onto fabric.

- -

You Will Need:

- Photo Transfer Paper for light fabrics
- White cotton sheeting/poplin
- Inkjet Printer
- Iron + Ironing Board

I use a photo paper to transfer my images onto fabric. Each photo gets printed out onto the paper and then transferred to white fabric using an iron. This fabric can then be stitched into your Stitchbook.

I find this is the method to use as the images are crisp and bright, and retain all of their detail even when printed at small sizes. However you can also use different methods including Imagemaker paste and printable fabric. Here i will just be describing how to use the photo transfer paper.

All of the images you want to use must be digital so that they can be printed, but you can scan in old photos using a home scanner.

You can also scan in and transfer hand written text, drawings, tickets or logos, to record even more information in your story.

HOW TO USE PHOTO TRANSFER PAPER

Printing

1. Chose your digital images and paste them onto a blank A4 document (I like to use Microsoft Publisher). You don't need to leave space between the images, in fact I try and squeeze as many on as I can to save paper! Re-size and crop each image as desired so they are the right size for your pages. You can print a test sheet on plain paper to check the sizes.

2. You need to reverse your images, because when they are printed they will be back-to-front.
   On Microsoft Office programs you select the photographs, then go to Picture Tools on the top menu bar and choose 'Flip Horizontal'.

   Other software may have a 'mirror mode' instead.

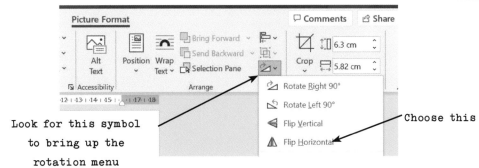

Look for this symbol to bring up the rotation menu

Choose this

3. Insert the transfer paper into the printer so that you can print onto the plain white side.

4. Print your document (you do not need to choose any special paper or ink settings).

Transfering

5. Cut out all of your images to separate them. Trim right to the edge of the photograph - they do not need a border around them.

6. Turn on your iron to heat up. Turn off the steam and use a medium heat (2 dots).*

7. Iron your white fabric to make sure it is flat. Remove any lint or stray threads as these will get trapped between the transfer and the fabric.

8. Place your transfer on the fabric, printed side down, (try and make sure the edges of the transfer follow the grain of the fabric).

9. Start ironing your image. Make sure all areas of the image receive the same amount of heat by moving the iron consistently in small circles, and covering all areas—especially the edges! Iron for about 60 seconds.

10. Leave the image to cool down— When cool, try to peel back one of the corners. If it does not appear to have transferred use the iron again for a longer time period or turn up the heat slightly*.

11. Peel the backing paper off.

Troubleshooting photo transfers:

Although I find them easy to use, there are several things that can go wrong when using transfers, mainly to do with the temperature. If you are struggling, look at the instructions that came with your paper. Here are also a few extra tips:

- Make sure you leave to cool completely before you peel off the backing.
- If the paper turns brown the iron is too hot.
- if the image is distorted or grainy the iron is too hot.
- If the image has bubbles in you haven't covered the whole image with heat.

*All irons will be slightly different temperatures. You will have to find the right setting for your iron. I suggest starting at a medium heat and then turning up if the image doesn't transfer fully.

ADDING TO YOUR STITCHBOOK

When you have transferred your image you have to decide how to attach it to your Stitchbook page.

You will need to trim the white cotton fabric of your photo to make the edges even, and it is a good idea to leave a 5mm border around the image.

The border means that when attaching it to your page, you will be sewing on the white fabric rather than the photo. This also frames your photograph with a nice white border, making it stand out from the rest of the content on your pages.

When stitching your photos:

Be aware that transferred pictures can shift when stitching and become crooked on the page - more so than when adding regular fabric due to the stiffness of the transfer.

To help:

- Pin within the white border of the image.
- Hold flat with one hand when stitching and go slowly.
- Use a temporary fix spray glue to hold the photo in place while you sew.

Remember! After you have transferred your photograph you cannot iron over the image or it will melt!

Options for adding to your page:

x x x x x x x x x x x

1. Sew with a machine zig-zag (set the width to the same size as the white part around your photo).

2. Stitch by hand - either an over edge whip stitch or blanket stitch to stop any fraying edges.

3. Use a felt photo frame and stitch this in place using a hand or machine stitch (see pg. 39).

4. Use a felt photo frame and brads (see pg. 40).

5. You can also cut the image so that it has no white border and you sew directly through the photograph. Be careful if you chose this method - not only will it obscure the edges of your image but the transfer can crack under the pressure of the needle.

MAKING A PHOTO FRAME WITH FELT

////////////////////////////

Using felt to frame your photos is an easy way to draw attention to the photograph and make a statement on the page.

- -

How to:

1. Transfer a photograph onto white cotton following the instructions on pg. 35.

2. Cut the photo out leaving a small white border. Place onto the middle of a piece of felt that is larger than you want the frame to be, and pin in place (pin around the white border to stop the pins making a hole in the surface of the photo).

3. Using a close zigzag stitch on the sewing machine, sew around the photo to secure it to the felt.

4. Cut around the photo leaving a felt border. Use pinking shears if you want a decorative border.

5. Attach by stitching onto the page (I like to use running stitch in embroidery thread) or with brads (see pg. 40).

Tip: It is best to do it this way round rather than cutting the felt to size, and then stitching, in case your photo moves while you are sewing it.

ATTACHING FELT FRAMES USING BRADS

//////////////////////////

A no-sew method!

- -

Brads are tiny metal pins that can be used to secure layers of paper or fabric together. They are a fancy type of split pin and have a round head with two long metal legs that splay out on the back of the fabric.

Brads come in lots of different sizes and colours and can also be found in exciting novelty shapes. Here I've used some small coloured brads so they fit in the small border between the photograph and the edge of the felt.

How to use:

1. Decide where your photo will go on the page.

2. Use a stitch unpick or sharp embroidery scissors to poke a small hole in one of the corners of the felt – just outside the machine stitching (don't cut through the stitching!).

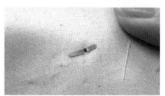

3. With the felt on top of the background in your desired position, poke a matching hole into the fabric through all layers.

4. Poke a brad through the hole and splay the legs on the back of the fabric (like a split pin). The brad should go through the felt layer, the background fabric and the Stitchbook page.

5. Repeat for all 4 corners.

OTHER PHOTO OPTIONS:

Transferring onto felt:

If you want to transfer a small image it is possible to transfer it onto felt instead of cotton. The felt is a good choice for small items because it doesn't fray and so can be cut in small or intricate patterns. Be careful which type of felt you use, it must be able to withstand the high temperatures of the iron, so any cheap polyester or acrylic felt may melt at this stage. I use a 40% wool felt which is happy with higher heat.

Using unusual shapes:

You can also cut your images into interesting shapes so they are not rectangular. Use circles or speech bubbles to create exciting designs or cut out a single figure from a photo. You can do this using photo editing software to change the shape before you print it - or just cut the paper out after printing. **Below** - after printing a photo onto transfer paper, I cut around the outline of my head then transferred to felt. This shape has then been cut out and stitched on the background.

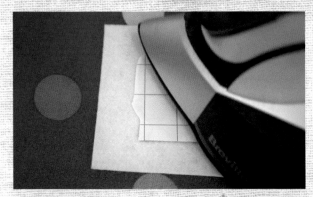

Using photo transfer paper to add text

On this page I have used the photo transfer paper to transfer writing from my typewriter onto the background fabric of the page. The text was written on the typewriter, then scanned into the computer and printed following the instructions on pg. 35. Each paragraph was transferred seperately.

XXX XXX

LETTERING

Index

ADDING TEXT

Text is integral to telling your story. Whether you are giving information (names, dates or places), adding description (what you did, felt or saw) or explaining the context of a photo, the Stitchbook wouldn't function without your words.

However, creating text for your Stitchbook is probably the hardest part of the whole project, as it can be fiddly, time consuming or need special equipment. I'm not going to pretend I can make it effortless, but this guide will hopefully give you some ideas and advice to make it more achievable.

All of the techniques here are ones I regularly use, and form the core way I use text in my Stitchbooks.

On the following pages I have outlined the technique, described the method I use to make and attach to my books, and also given you some examples and advice.

How to choose:

The main consideration when choosing which lettering method to use will be what materials you have and how big the lettering needs to be. For example, a title, which needs to be large on the page can't be made by rubber stamps if you've only got tiny sizes. Similarly, if you want to add a small label with a time and date then applique wouldn't be appropriate, as you won't be able to cut the pieces out small enough, let alone stitch them in place. Look at what equipment you have and match this to the size of text you need on each page.

It may also depend on how much time you are willing to spend on the project. Embroidery is a fantastic way to add large or small lettering but it is more time consuming than some of the other methods. Stamping is a good choice for a quicker project.

LETTER STAMPS

////////////////////////////////

Stamping is the quickest way to add text to your pages and the technique I use the most.

- -

All you need are a set of alphabet stamps and a regular black ink pad (this will be fine for fabric as long as you don't want to wash your book).

It is possible to stamp straight onto the fabric of your book, however I always stamp onto ribbon first, (rather than straight onto the page) and then stitch the ribbon into the book. This way if you go wrong (eg. the spacing is wonky or the edges are inky) you haven't ruined your page. You can just try again on another piece of ribbon.

How to stamp onto ribbon:

This is a very simple technique but you might need to practice to get it perfect. I recommend trying out new stamps on paper first to get familiar with the stamps.

1. Press the first letter of your word into the stamp pad (press very lightly or you'll get black marks on the edges).

2. Press the stamp onto the ribbon. Try and line up the stamp with a particular point on the ribbon so all of the stamps will be at the same height.

3.Continue stamping along the ribbon until all of your text is complete. Try and keep the spacing and height even (this is the most difficult bit!)

How to Attach To Your Stitchbook

Once they are all stamped and dry you can sew the ribbon onto your pages.

If the edges start to fray, tuck them under when you sew the ends, seal with the flame of a candle (if using a polyester ribbon), or use a dab of superglue or Fray-stop.

You can also stamp directly onto your book pages - but take care! If you go wrong you won't be able to change it!

Tips for Stamping

- -

- Press lightly into the ink pad to prevent build up of ink at the edges. I very lightly dab the stamp on the ink pad about five times, to ensure an even coat of ink.

- There are many types of ink and alphabet stamps available so try some different colours, sizes and fonts.

- Clean your stamps after use to make sure there isn't any wet ink left on them. Some ink will stay wet until the next time you use them which may cause colours to mix and messy edges in the future.

- You might find that sometimes the ink bleeds and becomes less clear when dry. Experiment with different combinations of ribbon and ink to find the ones that work best. A cotton tape can work well if it has a flat surface.

PRE-MADE STAMPS

/////////////////////////

Pre-made stamps are blocks that are made to show a specific design.

- -

These can be made of wood and rubber, or cling plastic which adheres to an acrylic block. These are usually designed to have mass appeal so have designs such as 'Happy Birthday' 'Wedding' or 'Congratulations'.

These are great if you can find the specific design that will suit your page themes.

I prefer to use the clear cling stamps as they come in a greater range of designs and you can see where you are stamping!

How to use Clear Cling Stamps:

1. Choose your design and stick to an acrylic block.

2. Press into an ink pad and stamp onto a piece of plain smooth fabric.

3. When dry, cut around the design

4. Stitch into your book. I use a zig-zag machine stitch or whip stitch to add make sure the edges don't fray.

Follow the tips on pg. 46 to achieve the best results.

Further Ideas: Use woven fabric instead of felt. Apply bondaweb to strengthen the fabric before cutting, then iron into place.

APPLIQUE

////////////////////////////////

Add texture and impact to your pages by using applique to cut and stitch letters made from felt.

- -

The easiest way of creating the letters is to use a computer to print out font templates, and this is the method I have outlined here. You will need to make these letters quite large (use for page titles only) or the felt will fall apart.

This method can be a bit fiddly but adds a fantastic depth and texture to your pages. I have added some tips to help you master it, and create your own bold titles.

You will need:

Felt

Computer printed lettering of your chosen title.

Small, sharp fabric scissors.

How to Applique letters using felt:

1. Choose a short word for your fabric title. Type the word out on the computer in your chosen font and print at the correct size for the space on your page.

2. Cut out the letter you want from the paper template.

3. Place the template onto felt and cut out the letter.

4. Place the felt letter onto the background and sew into place by stitching over the edge of the felt into the background using a whip stitch (see pg----)

5. Repeat with all letters.

(see pg----)

Applique Tips and Tricks:

- For letters with insides to cut out (a,o,p etc) cut these in stages. Cut around the paper template first, leaving the middle intact, then cut out this outline from felt. Next, cut out the middle of the paper shape and use this to cut the middle from the felt shape. This will give the paper shape more stability.

- Choose a simple, bold font. The best fonts to use are angular, sans serif fonts in upper case. Download new fonts to suit your project. These are usually free for home use and can be found at sites like Font Squirrel, DaFont and Fontspace.

- Use fine pointed embroidery scissors which are very sharp and can turn corners easily.

- Don't use pins—they can get in the way. Hold the paper and felt with one hand and cut with the other—turn as needed.

- If needed, use a glue stick to stick the template to the felt. Cut the letter out of paper then stick this (printed side down) to the back of the felt. Cut around then remove the paper.

EMBROIDERY

/////////////////////////

Hand embroidered lettering is a beautiful addition to any page. The only limit is your patience!

- -

I usually use embroidery to explain details of a special day or event, and to add name labels to photographs.

My favorite method is to hand write the text in an erasable pen (chose between heat, water or air erase pens which can be found in most craft stores) and use a back stitch to trace the lettering in embroidery thread.

Here I will be using a water erasable pen which disappears when water is added.

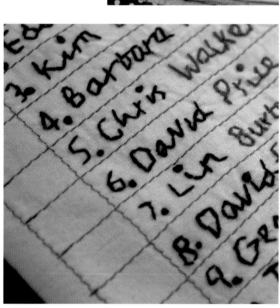

How to embroider using an erasable pen:

1. Use your erasable pen to write out your text onto your background fabric. You can use a ruler to draw guidelines to help you get it straight if you need to, but most of the time I like to embrace the natural wobbliness of hand writing.

2. Thread a needle with 1 or 2 strands of embroidery thread. How many you need will depend on how big your lettering is. The more strands of thread the chunkier your lettering will be.

3. Use a back stitch (see pg. 84) to sew the lettering, following along your drawn lines. Use small stitches around the curves to get smooth lines, and longer stitches for any straight lines.

4. When your embroidery is complete remove the pen according to the instructions (add water or heat or wait for it to disappear) .

(see pg. 84)

You will need:

An erasable fabric pen

Embroidery thread

Embroidery needle

Paintbrush or Iron depending on pen type.

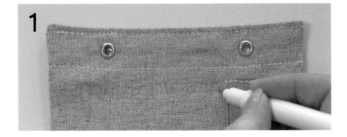

Experiment with:

- The size of your writing.
- The colour of your thread.
- The thickness of your embroidery thread.
- Different stitches - use a split stitch or chain stitch.
- Stitching onto different surfaces.
- Using all capital letters or all lower case.
- Tracing printed lettering as on pg. 53 and outline with stitching instead of paint.

FABRIC PAINT

////////////////////////////////

Trace computer printed fonts with fabric paint for unlimited text designs.

- -

Fabric Paint Tips and Tricks:

- For best results take your time and do several versions to see which one has the smoothest lines.

- You may need to add a little bit of water to your fabric paint to make it run smoothly (but not too much that it will bleed!)

- Use very smooth fabric with a tight weave to get your paint to cover evenly.

- Try using other fabric mediums such as fabric pens (thin-tipped Sharpies work well).

- Embellish with embroidery thread to highlight and underline words and decorate.

- Download new fonts to suit your project. These are usually free for home use and can be found at sites like Font Squirrel, DaFont and Fontspace.

- If you want to paint on opaque or dark surfaces, use an air erase pen (see pg. 51) to write out your word free hand and then paint over it.

How to trace lettering using fabric paint:

1. Create a template by writing your text on the computer and printing out at the desired size. I like to use a handwriting style font and print several sizes at once to see which is the best fit.

2. Place the template onto a light source (a light box or tape to a window) then place or tape the fabric on top.

3. Trace over the writing using fabric paint and a very fine brush. This takes practice to master, but go slowly and make sure your paint is the right consistency and you should be fine!

4. Leave the paint to dry then set to fix according to the fabric paint instructions (eg. with an iron).

5. Cut out your text. You can either cut it with a rotary cutter to create a rectangular block or use sharp fabric scissors to follow the outline of the lettering.

6. Stitch into your book. I use either a zig-zag machine stitch or a whip or blanket stitch to attach. This will control any fraying and create an attractive edge.

You will need:

Fabric paint

Smooth white cotton (easy to trace through)

Thin paintbrush

Light box (or bright window)

This page features two types of lettering: the names of my grandparents
have been hand embroidered, tracing my handwriting in back stitch. The
numbers have been stamped using clear cling stamps and a black ink pad.
I like to use several approaches to lettering on each page to keep things
interesting, especially on a page like this with little additional detail.

X X X X X X X X X X X

OTHER IDEAS

Planner Clips
Use clips designed for scrapbooks, bullet journals and planners. This one just clips to the top of the page.

Patches
Look for felt patches that have interesting phrases. These can be easily stitched onto the page.

Machine Embroidery.
Draw out an outline with an erasable pen then fill in using machine embroidery. Some sewing machines can also stitch computerised lettering.

Printed Fabric
This piece of quilting cotton was covered in phrases and images and I've just cut one out and added to the page.

Badges
Find Badges and enamel pins that express what you want to say. Simply pin to your pages.

DECORATION

Index

DECORATING YOUR PAGES

Decoration is the extra elements you add to your pages. They are not integral to the design or vital to telling your story, but they are the fun bits that make your books exciting to make and pleasing to look at.

When considering what decoration to add, think about why you are adding it.

The main reasons to add decoration are:

- To enhance your theme.
- Add texture
- Add colour or pattern.
- Add height and depth.
- Highlight specific areas or direct focus on the page

Some of the techniques in this chapter have been featured in previous sections, but they can be employed in different ways to be decorative rather than functional.

This is by no means an exhaustive list! Look out for anything that can be stitched or glued to your pages. This is a great opportunity to look through any craft materials accumulated through the years, and see if any can be used to create decorations. Think badges and patches, holiday souvenirs, logos cut from t-shirts and paper craft supplies such as scrapbooking embellishments and wooden shapes.

APPLIQUE

xxxxxxxxxx

In previous chapters I introduced using applique for backgrounds and for lettering. You can also use applique on top of the photo layer to add decoration.

There are several types of decorative applique:

1. Add blocks of fabric on top of the background or photos.

2. Cut out fabric shapes such as arrows, hearts and stars (felt works well for this).

3. Cut out motifs from fabric.

4. Select sections from clothing eg. part of a button placket of a shirt, a logo or a motif from baby grow.

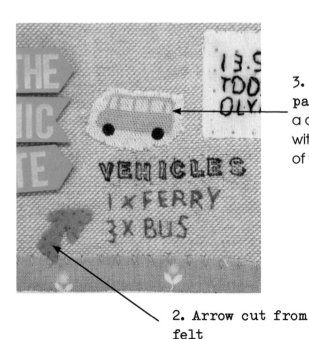

3. **Applique patch** - cut from a quilting fabric with lots of forms of transport.

2. **Arrow cut from felt**

4. **Pieces of Clothing**

This piece of embroidery was cut from an old childrens skirt. I love using old clothing because each piece has its own memories and nostalgia embedded, which gets transferred to your project.

Tip: You can also use Bondaweb to secure the fabric in place while you stitch - see pg. 62.

APPLIQUE PATCHES

////////////////////////////

Create patches from patterned fabric

- -

There are many gorgeous quilting fabrics that feature individual motifs such as flowers, figures or animals. These can be cut out and stitched into place. Look out for fabrics that match your theme or parts of your story.

How to make an applique patch:

1. Identify which part of the fabric you want to use. This could be a single icon or part of a larger pattern.

2. Cut around the image leaving a 5mm border (important as you will be sewing in this area).

3. Pin in place and stitch to the page using a machine, whip or blanket stitch. For best results, try to match the thread colour to the applique piece.

You will need:

Patterned fabric

Small sharp scissors

This page is almost entirely decorated with applique shapes. The background (behind the photos) are blocks of fabric. and I have also decorated the page with applique pieces - a strip of crosses and part of a group of pencils, both cut from larger fabric patterns. There are also shapes made from fabric paint (the heart, flower and banner) which have been cut out and stitched on.

MACHINE EMBROIDERY

//////////////////////////

Speed things up using a machine for freehand embroidery.

You can use machine embroidery to add shapes with stitched outlines. The double thickness of the Stitchbook pages make them very suited to machine embroidery as they are robust enough to be stitched into without a hoop.

Here I will show you how to do this with an applique background, but you could also just machine straight onto the page to create delicate lines of embroidery.

Left: This is a complicated example but shows that you can layer shapes using machine embroidery to create intricate multi-coloured images.

Further Ideas:

You can combine mulitiple techniques from this Handbook for extra wow factor!

Left: For these sunflowers I used a freezer paper stencil (pg. 24) to paint the flower shape on the background before using the machine to outline the petals and add a fabric center.

Machine embroidered applique:

1. Iron Bondaweb to the back of your fabric pieces.

2. Cut out shapes from the scraps. You can draw on the back of the Bondaweb paper or use a printed picture as a template.

3. Peel off the Bondaweb backing paper.

4. Iron the shapes onto your page in the desired place, Bondaweb side down, to fuse the fabric to the page.

5. Thread your machine with a contrasting colour and prepare it for free motion embroidery (eg. attach darning foot and lower feed dogs).

6. Stitch around the edge of the shape and along any decorative lines (here I have used both grey and white thread to add extra detail.)

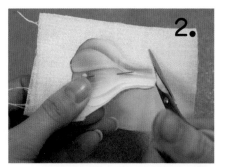

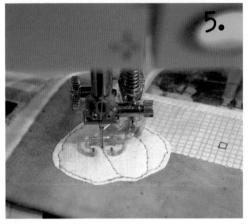

 This page shows you the garlic in context! I didn't have many photos of the actual garlic on the farm, so I needed to find another way to represent it. Using the machine to attach and outline the shape was a quick and simple way of doing this.

X X X X X X X X X X X

See pg. 84 for stitch diagrams and instructions

HAND EMBROIDERY

////////////////////////

Add decorative hand embroidery to add colour and texture to your pages.

- -

Experiment with a range of hand embroidery stitches, patterns and techniques. Stitch directly onto your page and through the background layers or onto fabric to be stitched in later (eg. cross stitch on aida). The only limit is your imagination, and patience!

You can achieve very different results by altering simple things:

1. Vary thread colour and try using variegated thread.
2. Change the thickness of your thread. The same stitch will look very different in six strands of thread rather than one.
3. Try out different types of stitch eg. cross stitch, running stitch, back stitch, seed stitch or chain stitch.
4. Explore line and patterns. Embroidery can be used to draw images as well as fill areas with texture and colour.

Left: A simple running stitch can form a decorative border around a photo.

Right: Seed stitch (here used with a slightly variegated thread) is a great filler for empty areas.

Arrow Patterns:

Create arrows with your thread to direct attention on the page.

Here are two form of arrows to try:

1. Use a back stitch to create chevrons. I have varied the colours to add extra interest.

2. Create a pattern of mini arrow shapes (each arrow created with three stitches, one forming the stem and two for the point).

Drawing with embroidery:
Draw out a picture using an erasable pen (pg. 51) and use a back stitch to trace your lines.

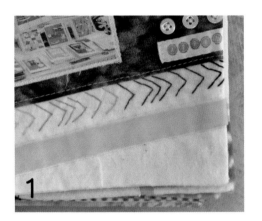

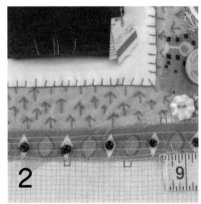

Stitching into Photo Paper:

Photo Transfers can also be stitched into using a sharp-pointed needle and a couple of strands of embroidery thread.

Be sparing with this- too much can crack the surface of the transfer.

On this image I have added some stars, crosses and french knots onto the girls dresses.

Follow the tips on pg. 46.

STAMPS AS DECORATION

////////////////////////

A quick and easy way to add complex detail.

- -

As well as being used for lettering, rubber and clear stamps can be helpful in adding decoration and complex shapes. They are available in a wide range of designs especially from companies focusing on scrapbooking. You can use coloured ink pads or fabric paint to vary the look of the designs. Also try stamping onto pastel or light coloured fabrics to create a coloured background.

Left: A stamped arrow leads the eye to the main element on the page.

Left: A stamped perpetual calander can be stitched on to show any date/s.

Above: This scrapbooking stamp has been printed onto white cotton and stitched to the page to express my thoughts on the photo.

This page features a number of stamps - From the blue and orange flowers, to the Hello Sunshine applique and even the tiny heart printed onto a scrap of pink and white ribbon. These have all been printed using clear cling stamps with an acrylic block and regular stamping ink. They have been printed onto either cotton fabric or cotton ribbon and hand stitched to the background using a whip stitch.

X X X X X X X X X X X

MINI ENVELOPES

///////////////////////////////

Felt envelopes are a useful way to add paper elements, and everyone will enjoy opening them to see what is inside.

Tip: You can change the size of the envelopes by printing the template at an enlarged or reduced scale.

- -

How to Make Felt Envelopes:

1. Scan and print, or photocopy, the template at the right size for your page (you might have to experiment to get this right!).

2. Pin the template to the felt and cut out.

3. Use an iron to press the flaps of the envelope towards the centre (test the temperature first so you don't melt the felt!). Fold the side flaps in to the centre and then fold the bottom flap up, and the top flap down.

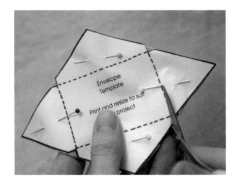

You will need:

A paper copy of the template on pg.85. Photocopy, trace or scan and print to the correct size.

Coloured felt

An iron

Embroidery thread

4. Stitch the bottom joins with small stitches using embroidery thread. (It is easiest to start at each corner and work towards the centre).

5. Stitch the envelope to your page at the edges.

RIBBON

///////////////////////////

Add colour and texture with beautiful ribbons .

- -

There are so many beautiful textured, coloured and patterned ribbons available, you are sure to be able to find ones to match and enhance your designs.

Ways to use ribbon:

1. Use long strips to divide pages, break the page into sections or tie areas of the page together.
2. Add to the bottom of pages as a fringe.
3. Use a group of ribbons to create a curtain of colour
4. Use velvet ribbon to add texture and make your page lovely to touch.

RIBBON TABS

///////////////////////////////

Add tabs to the top of your pages to help navigation.

- -

Ribbon tabs can be added between the folds of your Stitchbook pages to add extra detail (eg. years or sections) or to highlight specific important pages.

Fold the ribbon in half and hand stitch the raw ends to the inside of your page.

Ideas:

1. The tabs can be stamped or embroidered to add labels. The tabs in picture 1 show the year each of the pages features.

2. Make tabs from velvet ribbon to make it feel lovely to flick through the pages.

Tip: If you have a Cricut or Silhouette cutting machine you can use this to cut vinyl into text or compex shapes.

IRON-ON VINYL

///////////////////////////

A no-sew way to add decoration

- -

Iron-on vinyl is a special material that you can bond to fabric using an iron. It comes in a wide range of colours and textures, including glitter, flocked and holographic designs. Each brand of vinyl will have their own instructions and method of application, but I have outlined a broad overview below.

You will need:

A sheet of iron-on vinyl

Silicon coated paper

How to use iron-on vinyl:

1. Draw your design onto the back of the vinyl (usually the non-shiny side). Remember that the design will be reversed when adhered!

2. Cut around your drawing to create your vinyl shape.

3. Place on top of your chosen fabric or felt. Cover with a silicon coated sheet of paper and press with an iron according to the instructions that came with the vinyl.

4. Peel off the protective top layer of plastic film to reveal your design.

Above: Peeling off the protective top layer to reveal the vinyl. This star has been added to a piece of felt which will be cut around to create a sewable patch.

This page is a celebration of the rain! This was a very atmospheric walk so I wanted to reflect this in the decoration. Along with raincloud applique patches I have used 3 colours of blue vinyl to add a group of raindrops.

xxxxxxxxxxx

SEQUINS

////////////////////////////

Fill empty areas of your page with shiny sequins.

- -

Sequins are easy to sew on and come in a large range of sizes and colours. Position and attach each sequin to the page individually by stitching through the middle hole then out to the right and left sides.

Sequins can be positioned in a line, scattered over the page or grouped in a specific area of the page to create a pattern. This pattern is a great way to fill empty areas of the page and to add texture and sparkle.

Left: Use novelty shaped sequins to enhance a themed page.

Right: I have used a series of sequins to fill in this fabric painted number.

EMBELLISHMENTS

There are a lot more ways to embellish your pages than I have covered, here are a few more examples of things you can use:

Plastic or Card Shapes

Use scrapbook supplies, like these perspex shapes. Fabric glue will easily stick them to the page.

Badges and Patches

Be on the look out for useful badges and patches to add to your book. These could be souvenirs from places you visit, your old guide/scout/swimming badges, or designs from small businesses.

Special Buttons

These flower buttons are ceramic and I bought them from the maker at a craft fair. It is nice use embellishments with memories or meaning attached.

Lace/Doilies

Vintage lace and table linen can be used to add charm to a page and help celebrate a special moment like a wedding or christening.

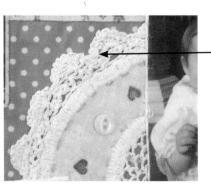

PUTTING IT ALL TOGETHER

Index

PUTTING IT ALL TOGETHER:

This section is about how you can put all of the techniques mentioned in this Handbook together to form your page designs.

The techniques I have used are often quite simple on their own, but the magic comes when you combine them on a page. For best results, aim for multiple layers of fabric, overlapping elements and to include a range of techniques per page.

Feeling overwhelmed by the possibilities? Think about what you need to add to be able to tell your story. Consider what the most important part of the page is and how you can direct focus towards that part. Do you want to highlight a photo, the title or another bit of information. What techniques can you use that will make that part stand out? This might be giving a photo a bright and colourful frame (pg. 39), creating a bold applique title (pg. 48) or adding directional arrows using embroidery to guide the eye towards a certain point (pg. 65).

Remember there are no limits or restrictions to what you add and you can continue to add to the pages over time - just remove the page from the binding rings to continue stitching.

In this chapter I have included a run through of the order I add my elements in, plus a couple of sample pages with the different parts of the design labelled. I have explained the processes involved and decisions such as the choice of colours. I have also included the page numbers in the examples, aso you can easily look up the details of the techniques.

HOW TO DECORATE A PAGE:

You can decorate your pages however you like, but to get you started here is a run through of the process that I typically use. All of the fabrics get added onto the background in layers, to build up the decoration and detail.

1. Print out your photographs and transfer to fabric using the method on pg. 35 . Decide on your page colour scheme and find some fabric and embelishments that will compliment the photo and story.

2. Refer to your planning sheet to know which page to decorate (left or right side). Take the page out of the binding rings and lay flat. This is where you are going to stitch your page design.

3. Cut small pieces from your chosen fabrics and lay onto the page. Decide on an arrangement and sew onto the background using a sewing machine or by hand.

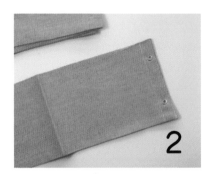

4. Place your fabric photographs on the page and pin in the white cotton border around the edge of the photograph. Sew into place using a machine zigzag. Try and keep your stitches within the white border.

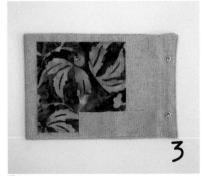

5. Add a strip of ribbon to add colour and texture. I have used a purple grosgrain ribbon and stitched this on by hand.

6. Add your text. Here I have used lettering stampers for the names and embroidery thread for the title. The names have been stamped onto thin white ribbon and hand stitched to the background. The embroidery thread was stitched over an erasable pen written in my handwriting.

7. Add embellishments to add detail to the page.

Button

Sequins

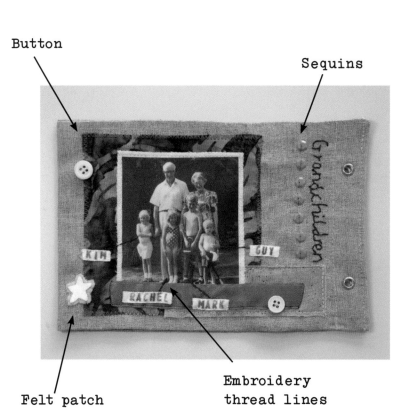

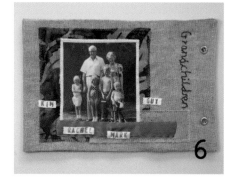

Felt patch

Embroidery thread lines

8. When you have finished adding your details, fold the page back in half and re-insert binding rings.

Things to remember:

- Unfold the page every time you sew
- Don't sew over the eyelet holes.
- You can leave parts of the background blank.

EXAMPLE PAGES:

Sequins applied within a patchwork block to form a decorative pattern.

These names were stamped onto thin ribbon using blue ink (pg. 45).

Photo framed with glitter felt edged with pinking shears (pg. 39).

Note: This double page spread is from a slightly different form of Stitchbook (which is made without binding rings) but the main construction points are the same.

Perpetual calendar stamp - A clear cling stamp and black ink with added embroidery (pg. 47).

Hand printed fabric using wooden blocks and fabric paint (pg. 23).

Applique lettering cut from glitter felt and hand stitched in place (pg. 48).

The backgrounds were pieced together by machine before stitching onto the page (pg. 28).

Extra details made with clear cling stamps and black ink. Printed onto white cotton and stitched on by hand (pg. 47).

Hand printed fabric using wooden blocks and fabric paint (pg. 23).

Colour scheme: This was a craft fair that I had a stall at during the hottest weekend of the year. The yellow and blue colours were designed to represent the blue sky and ever-present sun.

RAINBOW ROLLER SKATES

Ribbon applied along the raw edge of the fabric block.

Photo machine stitched to a felt frame and secured with 4 colours of brads (pg. 40).

Found decoration: Rainbow badge pinned to fabric and blue arrow patch stitched on.

Text written on typewriter then scanned in and transferred to fabric (pg. 42).

My brief stint as a rollerskater before falling over, doing my back in and deciding i'm too fragile to be throwing myself around on wheels.

A SURPRISE BIRTHDAY PRESENT FROM GUY

Ribbons to match the colours on the main fabric. Folded ends stitched to the page (pg. 70).

Text stamped onto thin ribbon using black ink (pg. 45).

Flower stencil made from freezer paper with yellow fabric paint (pg. 24) with a centre made from machine embroidery on top of an orange applique circle (pg. 61).

Buttons add a vibrant yellow to mimic the sunflowers in the photos.

Background has been quilted with rows of straight machine stitching.

Text stamped onto white felt using sepia coloured ink (pg. 45).

Colour scheme: The colours of the fabric and decoration were chosen to mimic those in the photos, which match my memories of the day they were taken .

STITCH DIAGRAMS

Whip Stitch for Applique

Bring your needle up at point 1, 5 mm in from the edge of the felt letter. Put the needle down just over the edge, into the main body fabric (point 2). Come up again to the on the fabric patch (point 3) and repeat.

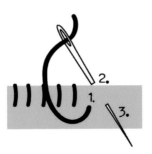

Back Stitch

Make 1 stitch at the start of your stitching line. Then bring your needle up ahead of this stitch (point 1). Put your needle back into the end of the last stitch (point2) to complete a solid line.

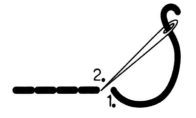

Seed Stitch

The idea of seed stitch is to create the impression of random stitches that still look pleasing. Create stitches of even size that face in different directions,

Chain Stitch

Bring the thread out at point 1. Put the needle down at point 2 and bring the needle up at point 3; don't pull through yet! Place the working thread behind the needle as shown, creating a loop. Pull the needle through the loop.

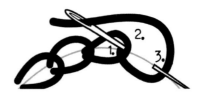

TEMPLATES AND PRINTABLES

Scan and print these at your desired size.

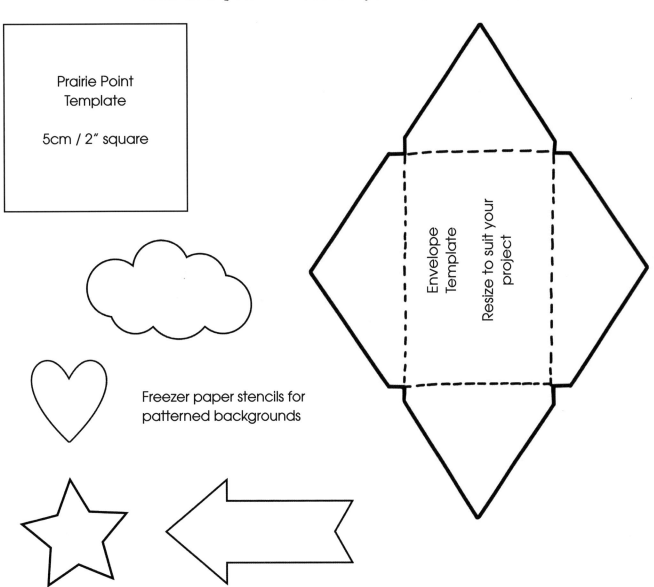

Prairie Point
Template

5cm / 2" square

Freezer paper stencils for
patterned backgrounds

Envelope
Template

Resize to suit your
project

RESOURCES

My favourite suppliers, many of their products have been used throughout this book.

Billow Fabrics

Quilting fabrics and wool felt.

www.billowfabrics.co.uk

Bramble Fox

Perspex scrapbook shapes

www.bramblefox.co.uk

ClothKits

Quilting fabric and haberdashery

www.clothkits.co.uk

Eternal Maker

Quilting fabric and haberdashery

eternalmaker.com

Happy Fabric

Iron-on vinyl, heat presses and cutters.

www.happyfabric.co.uk

Helen Steele

Screen printed fabrics

helen-steele.com

Kate Holliday

Decorative ceramic buttons

www.kateholliday.co.uk

Miesje Chafer

Print on demand fabric pattern library

www.miesjechafer.com

Mint Maker Studio

Clear stamps including custom designs.

www.mintmakerstudio.co.uk

Pick Pretty Paints

Hand mixed printing paints.

www.pickprettypaints.com

Studio Calico

Scrapbook and stamping supplies

www.studiocalico.com

Wool Felt Company

Wool and handmade felt.

www.woolfeltcompany.co.uk

OTHER PUBLICATIONS

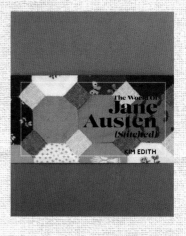

Stitch your Family Story

Ideas for telling your family history in fabric.

Stitchbooking: An Introduction- Zine

A brief outline of the craft of Stitchbooking.

The World of Jane Austen (Stitched)

Fabric illustrations of the recurring themes in Jane Austen's work.

ABOUT THE AUTHOR:

Kim Edith is a textile artist based in the Hotwalls Studios, Portsmouth. She trained as an illustrator at Kingston University before falling in love with fabric and turning from pencil to thread as a way to create images. Kim explores narrative through textiles, using mixed media collage to create fabric books, art quilts and collections of themed illustrations.

Kim likes museums, vintage toys and going on day trips.

©Kim Burton 2022

Published by Stitchbook Studio Press

Studio 6, Hotwalls, Broad Street, Portsmouth, PO1 2FS

Printed and bound by ExWhyZed

ISBN 9781739831714

First published 2022

www.stitchbookstudio.com

 @kimedith

 @stitchbookstudio